Robert Quackenbush

OLD SILVER LEG TAKES OVER!

A Story of Peter Stuyvesant

•

Prentice-Hall, Inc.

ENGLEWOOD CLIFFS, NEW JERSEY

Stuyvesant

Printed in Spain by Novograph, S.A., Madrid   ·J
Prentice-Hall International (UK) Limited, London
Prentice-Hall of Australia, Pty. Ltd., Sydney
Prentice-Hall Canada, Inc., Toronto
Prentice-Hall Hispanoamericana, S.A., Mexico
Prentice-Hall of India Private Ltd., New Delhi
Prentice-Hall of Japan, Inc., Tokyo
Prentice-Hall of Southeast Asia Pte. Ltd., Singapore
Whitehall Books Limited, Wellington, New Zealand
Editora Prentice-Hall do Brasil LTDA., Rio de Janeiro

10 9 8 7 6 5 4 3 2 1

Library of Congress Cataloging-in-Publication Data

Quackenbush, Robert.
  Old Silver Leg takes over.

  Summary: A brief biography of the Dutchman who
arrived to be governor of New Amsterdam in 1647 and
turned that city from a muddy village into a well-
organized city.
  1. Stuyvesant, Peter, 1592-1672—Juvenile
literature.   2. New York (State)—Governors—
Biography—Juvenile literature.   3. Dutch—New York
(State)—History—17th century—Juvenile literature.
4. New York (State)—History—Colonial period,
ca. 1600-1775—Juvenile literature.   5. New York
(N.Y.)—History—Colonial period, ca. 1600-1775—
Juvenile literature.   [1. Stuyvesant, Peter, 1592-1672.
2. Governors.   3. New York (N.Y.)—History—Colonial
period, ca. 1600-1775]   I. Title.
F122.1.S78Q33   1986   974.7'02'0924   [B] [92] 85-25661
ISBN 0-13-633934-4

For Piet

and with special thanks to the librarians at
The Holland Society of New York

There was once a boy named Peter Stuyvesant, who was born in Holland in the year 1592. No one knows the exact date of his birth. He was the son of a poor preacher. He had an older sister named Anna who was quiet and reserved. But Peter was not quiet! He would stomp and shout and make a big fuss. When Anna had had enough of his wild ways, she would tell him to be still. Peter would listen for the moment because he looked up to his sister. Then he would go right back to being the way he was, which was forever playing soldier or pretending he was the commander of a magnificent Dutch ship. It was obvious to everyone in the family that he was headed for an adventurous life.

9

In 1602, while Peter was still in school, the great Dutch East India Company was formed. All of Holland's traders joined this company, hoping to keep trade with the East Indies in Dutch hands. The Company wanted to find a route to the Indies that would be shorter than the long journey around Africa's Cape of Good Hope. So in 1609 they sent the ship *Half Moon*, commanded by Henry Hudson, to look for a "Northwest Passage" through North America to the Pacific. Of course, Hudson did not find a "Northwest Passage" because it doesn't exist. However, he made other important discoveries, including what are now called the Hudson River and Manhattan Island. His discoveries led to the formation in 1621 of another company—the Dutch West India Company—for trading on the western coast of Africa, in the West Indies, and on the eastern coast of America. Just the place for a young man with his eyes set on adventure! So no one was surprised, least of all his mother, father and sister, when Peter Stuyvesant took the position of clerk with the Dutch West India Company after he finished school.

UH, OH! HERE COMES TROUBLE!

Stuyvesant was ambitious and determined to do well in the Dutch West India Company. His hard work did not go unnoticed. Soon he was sent to manage several trading posts in Brazil. His success there led to his appointment as governor of Curaçao, an island off the coast of what is now Venezuela. However, Stuyvesant stayed there for only eighteen months. During a battle with the Portuguese on the island of Saint Martin, Stuyvesant, the commander, was hit in the right leg by a wayward cannonball. His leg was so badly crushed that it had to be removed and buried in Curaçao. Stuyvesant returned to Holland for further treatment, where he was fitted with a wooden leg that was decorated with silver. He stayed with his sister, who was now married and had three children. The visit was a success, for although he had lost a leg, he gained a wife. His bride was the sister of his brother-in-law. Her name was Judith Bayard.

12

Meanwhile, the Dutch had not neglected their territories in the New World. They bought Manhattan Island from the peaceful Indians who lived there, for sixty guilders (twenty-four dollars in nineteenth-century currency) in pretty cloth, hatchets, needles, fish hooks and other trifles. A fort and a few houses were built on the island, and the little settlement was called New Amsterdam. But it needed settlers. So the Dutch West India Company decided to give a free piece of land to any Dutchman who would pay for fifty or more people to go there. These landowners were called patroons. Many of them never traveled to see their land, but they were eager to own it anyway because they expected the settlement to grow and prosper. However, New Amsterdam did have some problems, especially with its governors. Two men had tried and failed to do the job. The latest governor, William Kieft, had been the worst. He had even provoked a war with the Indians that lasted for five years. So the Dutch West India Company offered the job to Peter Stuyvesant. *And was he happy!*

14

I LOVE TO TRAVEL.

YES, FROM ONE MUD HOLE TO THE NEXT.

But not for long. When the new governor arrived in New Amsterdam in 1647 with his wife, his recently widowed sister, and her three children, he was horrified. Instead of streets of gold—as he expected—he saw mud. The walls of Fort Amsterdam were used as grazing fields for a couple of cows. Chickens made their nests under the mouths of the fort's rusty cannons. Of the three windmills, one could no longer be used, while a second one had burned down. The houses were clumsily built of wood, with thatched roofs and wooden chimneys. The town's outhouses were set directly on the street, creating unpleasant odors. Pigs wandered about at will, kept out of vegetable gardens only by rough stockades. The church was unfinished. There were 150 dwellings and one quarter of them were taverns. There was drunkenness and fighting in the streets, even on the Sabbath which was supposed to be a day of quiet and prayer. Stuyvesant had a lot to do.

17

Stuyvesant got his family settled in the governor's house, which was one of the few stone buildings in the city. Then he set to work. He insisted that all taverns close one hour earlier—at nine in the evening—and fined people for knife-throwing, brawling in the streets, and Sunday drinking. He ordered pens to be built for the pigs and outhouses removed from the streets. He demanded that chimneys be inspected and their owners taxed if they were unsafe. Then, to raise money to repair the crumbling fort, he made people pay a tax on imported liquors and wines. All this made him unpopular and some of the citizens threatened that they would protest to the West India Company in Holland. However, Stuyvesant knew how to respond to the rabble-rousers. He stomped his peg leg and barked, "If anyone during my administration shall appeal, I will make him a foot shorter, and send the pieces to Holland and let him appeal in that way."

19

Then Stuyvesant went up the Hudson River to inspect another Dutch settlement called Fort Orange (now the city of Albany). There he found that the village of Beverwyck, which had nestled on Company land right next to the fort for protection, was interfering with the use of the fort. Some of the village rooftops were too high and prevented the firing of the cannons. Stuyvesant stomped his peg leg and ordered the homes to be torn down. But the agent for the patroon who owned the land where the houses stood refused to carry out the order. A violent quarrel erupted. Even the nearby Indians could not understand why "Old Silver Leg" wanted to pull down his countrymen's houses. Stuyvesant angrily went home. Then he sent a small army of soldiers from Manhattan to carry out his orders. But the soldiers met so much opposition from the outraged inhabitants that they had to turn around and go back home. With that, Stuyvesant threw up his hands and returned to his problems in New Amsterdam.

21

Gradually, during the first years of Stuyvesant's leadership, New Amsterdam became a little more orderly. Many new settlers flocked there from Holland. The damage done by the Indian war was repaired. Dutch trading ships crowded the harbor. But with prosperity, the people grew restless under the rule of the Dutch West India Company with Stuyvesant as the Company representative. They longed for the political liberties they had had in Holland. In 1653, Adriaen Van der Donck—the first lawyer to settle in New Netherland—went to Holland to ask for changes from the high office of States-General. He returned victorious. The Company was obliged to give in. The government of New Amsterdam was to have—in addition to Stuyvesant as director-general—two burgomasters (mayors), five schepens (heads of districts), and a schout (sheriff), just like the towns in Holland. What could Stuyvesant do? Orders were orders. He stomped his peg leg and shouted and fussed at first. Then he relented. And he did manage to fill the new offices with men he had chosen.

22

Stuyvesant and his burgomasters and schepens met in a large stone building—a former tavern—which was called the Stadt-Huys (like our word "State House"). There they set to work to answer complaints and to settle disputes among the citizens. One dispute was the case of Wolfer Webber and his neighbor Judith Verleth. Webber complained that Judith had been pestering him. He claimed that she had come over to his house the week before to beat him; afterward she threw stones at him. Judith admitted that she had done this because Webber had called her names and once threatened to strike her with a broom. The parties were ordered to keep away from each other and Webber was fined for telling a lie during the meeting. In another case, Messack Martens stole cabbages from Pieter Jansen. Martens was ordered to stand in the town square with cabbages on his head. There were also cases of slander. Pieter Pieterson Smit called Joghem Beeckman a "black pudding" and Isaac Bealo called Joost Goderis a "horned beast." The name-callers were fined. And so it went all day long.

25

In addition to settling disputes, Stuyvesant and his council passed laws. Some of the first laws had to do with fire safety. All fire hazards such as wooden chimneys, thatched roofs, haystacks, henhouses, and pigpens within the town were ordered to be removed. Each house, great or small, paid a tax of one beaver skin to pay for fire buckets, ladders, and hooks in case of fire. Thus began the first fire department in America. Another law was passed to provide a home for the poor and one for orphans. Also, a secondary school was established. No longer did children have to attend makeshift classes in noisy taverns. At last the town was taking shape. Stuyvesant's dream was being realized. Still, this didn't stop him from stomping his peg leg and shouting and making a fuss when things didn't go his way. Often his sister silenced him when he went too far, just as she had done when they were children. She had a way of accomplishing what Stuyvesant's devoted wife and two sons, Balthazar and Nicholas, would never think of doing.

26

In 1653, war broke out between England and Holland. At once, Stuyvesant began construction of a wall at the north edge of town, from the East River across to the Hudson River, to keep out the enemy. It was a wall of wood, twelve feet high, with a sloping platform inside. Soldiers could climb on the platform and look over the wall for approaching enemies. The soldiers on guard made a path along the wall and this became known as "Wall Street." At one end of the wall was a gate near the East River. At the western end was a gate to a country road that led to Boston, called Breede Weg (now Broadway). But the enemy never came and war with the English didn't seem likely, so the townspeople stopped giving money to build the wall. But Stuyvesant was determined to finish it. He spent money from his own pocket and asked for donations from wealthier citizens. While he had wanted to build a wall around the whole town, he was satisfied that at least one portion of it was built.

CAN YOU BELIEVE THIS? FIRST THEY FENCE US IN. THEN THEY MOVE US OUT OF TOWN. FINALLY, THEY FENCE THEMSELVES IN.

THEY SHOULD HAVE DONE THE LAST THING FIRST, LOCKED THEMSELVES IN AND THROWN AWAY THE KEY.

New Amsterdam by the 1660s had changed greatly from its early days. Its streets were paved with brick. It had 350 brick houses with tile roofs. Its population numbered 1400 and over eighteen different languages were spoken. Goods from all over the world were traded in the marketplace next to the fort (now called Bowling Green). The town was on its way to becoming one of the most successful intellectual and financial centers of the world. Not only that, Stuyvesant nurtured the growth of other nearby Dutch settlements at Fort Casimir on the Delaware River and at Fort Orange. These settlements, together with others in what are now New Jersey, Pennsylvania, Connecticut, and southern New York State, made up Holland's territory in North America and it was called New Netherland. They prospered as rapidly as New Amsterdam. Stuyvesant's administration had done well. But it was all to end soon. Too soon.

31

The war had continued between Holland and England. Suddenly, on September 5, 1664, four English ships carrying 450 soldiers came into the harbor of New Amsterdam and invaded Long Island. New Amsterdam was defenseless. The fort was unprepared and the wall north of the town was useless because the enemy was coming from the south and east. Stuyvesant received a letter from the English commander who said he must surrender or face bombardment of the town. He tore up the letter and stomped on the pieces with his peg leg. "I'd rather go to my grave!" he shouted. He planned to keep the letter a secret so the townspeople would fight. But his Council did not want to risk bloodshed. In haste, the burgomasters and schepens and the schout pieced and pasted the letter back together as best they could and had it read before the people. The principal citizens urged Stuyvesant to surrender. Stuyvesant had no choice but to hoist a white flag above the fort. The next day, all of New Netherlands was surrendered to the English. And New Amsterdam became New York.

After the surrender, Stuyvesant was ordered to return to Holland at once and explain to the Dutch West India Company how he had lost their valuable land and settlements. When he arrived, he gave the angry leaders of the Company some letters from his Council. All the letters told of his bravery and insisted that he could have done nothing more during the invasion by the English. "His Honour," said one letter, "hath during eighteen years administration, conducted himself as he ought to do for the best interests of the West India Company." After reading the letters, the Company pardoned Stuyvesant. He returned to New Amsterdam, to his family and his home. He brought with him a pear tree which he planted near his house; it stood firm for nearly 200 years until it was blown down by a storm. The great former Director-General spent his remaining years puttering in his garden and living a quiet life with his family. From all accounts, he never stomped his peg leg or shouted or fussed again.

Epilogue

In 1673, just one year after the death of Peter Stuyvesant at the age of eighty, Dutch sailors again hoisted Holland's flag on Manhattan Island. They sailed into the harbor and took the English by surprise. The fort surrendered unconditionally; the English marched out and the Dutch moved in. But the takeover lasted for only fifteen months. In 1674 a peace treaty was signed between England and Holland, and New Netherland became permanently New York. However, its population remained largely Dutch until nearly 1750. The language and customs of Holland survived until recent years in a few villages on Long Island, in New Jersey, and along the Hudson River. The early Dutch methods of governing by council were adapted by our forefathers when the United States became a free and independent nation. Those first Dutch settlers contributed much to our country. Today, streets and towns with Dutch names remind us of the man with the wooden leg who ruled New Amsterdam. Would he have been surprised to see how his little town of 150 houses has grown into the huge metropolis of New York City?